Character Education

Generosity

by Lucia Raatma

Consultant:
Madonna Murphy, Ph.D.
Professor of Education
University of St. Francis, Joliet, Illinois
Author, *Character Education in America's
Blue Ribbon Schools*

Bridgestone Books
an imprint of Capstone Press
Mankato, Minnesota

Bridgestone Books are published by Capstone Press
151 Good Counsel Drive, P.O. Box 669, Mankato, Minnesota 56002
http://www.capstone-press.com

Library of Congress Cataloging-in-Publication Data
Raatma, Lucia.
    Generosity / by Lucia Raatma.
       p. cm.—(Character education)
    Summary: Explains the virtue of generosity and describes ways to show it in the home,
school, and community.
    Includes bibliographical references and index.
    0-7368-1388-8 (hardcover)
1. Generosity—Juvenile literature. [1. Generosity.] I. Title. II. Series.
BJ1533.G4 R32 2003
179'.9—dc21   2001007904

Editorial Credits

Megan Schoeneberger, editor; Karen Risch, product planning editor; Steve Christensen,
    series designer, Heidi Meyer, book designer; Alta Schaffer, photo researcher;
    Nancy White, photo stylist

Photo Credits

Capstone Press/Jim Foell, cover, 4, 6, 8, 12, 14, 16, 20
Clara Barton National Historic Site, National Park Service, 18
Norvia Behling, 10

1 2 3 4 5 6 07 06 05 04 03 02

Table of Contents

Generosity

Generosity is about giving to others. It means sharing with the people around you. It is about seeing when others need help. A generous person is happy to give. Generosity means not expecting anything in return.

Titles in this series:
My ABCs   Mo
My Counting Book Birds
Bugs A to Z   How M

Being Generous

Generosity is not just about giving gifts or money. Even a person without money can be generous. You can be generous by giving your time. Read to a younger cousin. Visit older neighbors. Listen to a friend who is upset.

Generosity at Home

Generosity means giving your time to help your family. You can offer to do the dishes. A generous person shares with others. Share your toys with your siblings. Let them choose a video to watch.

sibling
a brother or a sister

Generosity with Your Friends

A generous person does thoughtful things for others throughout the year. You can give gifts to your friends on holidays or birthdays. You can send them a card when they are sad or worried.

Generosity at School

School is an important place to be generous. A generous person helps the teacher straighten desks after class. You can share a sandwich with someone who has forgotten to bring lunch. You also can be generous by spending time with a new student.

Generosity in Sports

Generosity is an important part of sportsmanship. A generous person plays as part of a team. You can pass the ball instead of always taking the shot. Being generous means praising a teammate after a good play. A generous person congratulates the winner.

sportsmanship

playing a sport or game respectfully and fairly

Generosity in Your Community

Generous people help others in their community. You can volunteer to help others. Bring food and clothing to people who need them. Help care for animals at the local shelter.

volunteer

to offer to do a job without pay

"The Red Cross is a part of us—it has come to stay—and like the sturdy oak, its spreading branches shall yet encompass and shelter the relief of the nation."
—Clara Barton

Generosity and Clara Barton

Clara Barton was a nurse during the Civil War (1861–1865). She took care of many hurt and sick soldiers. The soldiers called her "the angel of the battlefield." Clara helped start the Red Cross in the United States.

Red Cross
an organization that gives food, clothing, and money to people after floods, earthquakes, war, and other terrible events

Generosity and You

Some people will have more money or things than you have. Some people will have less. Being generous means giving what you can to others. You can feel good about yourself when you are generous.

Hands On: Hold a Clothing Drive

Many people could use clothing that you no longer need. Hold a clothing drive at your school. Collect items for a local shelter to show your generosity.

What You Need

An adult
Paper
Markers
Large boxes or bags

What You Do

1. Talk to your teacher or another adult about starting a clothing drive.
2. Have the adult check with a local shelter. Make sure the shelter can accept the clothing. The shelter may give you ideas and instructions for your clothing drive.
3. Use the paper and markers to make posters. Ask people to bring used clothing that is clean and in good condition. Tell them when and where to bring the clothing.
4. Collect the clothing in large boxes or bags.
5. Ask an adult to drive the clothing to the shelter.
6. Remember to thank everyone who helps.

Words to Know

congratulate (kuhn-GRACH-uh-late)—to tell someone that you are pleased because he or she has done something well

praise (PRAZE)—to use positive words about a person's actions or appearance

shelter (SHEL-tur)—a safe place where a homeless person, a victim of a disaster, or an animal that is not wanted can stay

sibling (SIB-ling)—a brother or a sister

Read More

Francis, Dorothy Brenner. *Clara Barton: Founder of the American Red Cross.* A Gateway Biography. Brookfield, Conn.: Millbrook Press, 2002.

Lingo, Susan L. *101 Simple Service Projects Kids Can Do.* Cincinnati: Standard Publishing, 2000.

Internet Sites

Kids Can Make a Difference
http://www.kids.maine.org
Kids Care Clubs
http://www.kidscare.org/kidscare/index.htm
National Women's Hall of Fame—Clara Barton
http://www.greatwomen.org/profile.php?id=17

Index